NORTHWOOD
KING OF CARNIVAL GLASS

by

Bill Edwards

COLLECTOR BOOKS
A Division of Schroeder Publishing Co., Inc.

The current values in this book should be used only as a guide. They are not intended to set prices, which vary from one section of the country to another. Auction prices as well as dealer prices vary greatly and are affected by condition as well as demand. Neither the Author nor the Publisher assumes responsibility for any losses that might be incurred as a result of consulting this guide.

Additional copies of this book may be ordered from:

COLLECTOR BOOKS
P.O. Box 3009
Paducah, Kentucky 42001

@$9.95 Add $1.00 for postage and handling.

Copyright: Bill Schroeder & Bill Edwards, 1978
ISBN: 0-89145-070-X

Printed by IMAGE GRAPHICS, Paducah, Kentucky

ACKNOWLEDGEMENTS

My grateful thanks to the following people for their aid in this book. What a wonderful bunch of people carnival glass collectors are!

The Jim Capps	Nancy Williams
The Bert Newmans	The Larry Yungs
The Robert McCaslins	Mrs. Peugh
The Terry Henrys	C.B. Carroll
Norma Morrison	The Jim Warrens
Thelma Harmon	The Harold Ludemans
The Howard Battins	Rick Kojis
June Germann	Thomas Ledbetter
The Gordon Williams	Ken Abendroth
Lee Markley	Chester Herring
David Hunt	Tom Burns
The Carl Bookers	Rovene Heaton
The Herb Ripleys	The Carlton Schleedes
The Jerry Hunters	The Bob Leonards
Glenn VanZante	

And, of course, a very special thanks to Mr. William Heacock for sharing the Dugan shards and the Hoosier Carnival Glass Association who came to my rescue with their glass to be photographed when I needed them. And finally, my typist, Doris Kabel.

God Bless All of You!

DEDICATION

In memory of my father, Russell Edwards, and for the three young loves of my life, Kimberly, Pamela and Michael Edwards.

THE NORTHWOOD STORY

An entire book could be written about Harry Northwood, using every superlative the mind could summon and still fail to do justice to the man; a genius in his field.

Of course Harry had an advantage in the glass industry since his father, John Northwood, was a renowned English glass maker.

Harry Northwood came to America in 1880 and first worked for Hobbs, Brockunier and Company of Wheeling, West Virginia, an old and established glass producing firm. For five years Harry remained in Wheeling, learning his craft and dreaming his dreams.

In 1886, he left Hobbs, Brockunier and became employed by the Labelle Glass Company of Bridgeport, Ohio, where he advanced to the position of Manager in 1887. A few months later a devastating fire destroyed much of the LaBelle factory and it was sold in 1888.

Harry next went to work for the Buckeye Glass Company of Martin's Ferry, Ohio. Here he remained until 1896 when he formed the Northwood Company at Indiana, Pennsylvania. Much of the genius was now being evidenced and such products as the famous Northwood custard glass date from this period.

In 1899 Northwood entered the National Glass combine only to become unhappy with its financial problems and in 1901 he broke away to become an independent manufacturer once again.

A year later, he bought the long-idle Hobbs, Brockunier plant and for the next couple of years there were two Northwood plants.

Finally, in 1904, Northwood leased the Indiana, Pennsylvania plant to its managers, Thomas E. Dugan and W. G. Minnemeyer, who changed the name of the plant to the Dugan Glass Company (in 1913 the plant officially became known as the Diamond Glass Company and existed as such until it burned to the ground in 1931).

In 1908, Harry Northwood, following the success of his student, Frank L. Fenton, in the iridized glass field, marketed his first Northwood iridescent glass and Northwood carnival glass was born. For a ten year period, carnival glass was the great American "craze" and even at the time of Harry Northwood's death in 1921, small quantities were still being manufactured. It had proved to be Northwood's most popular glass, the jewel in the crown of a genius, much of it marked with the well-known trade-mark.

In July, 1977, I was permitted to sort through the shards of the 1975 Helman diggings at the old Dugan dump site in Indiana, Pennsylvania.

These shards were made available to me by William Heacock, noted author of Victorian Pattern glass books. The gesture was not only unique in the field of glass research, but generous beyond belief, for it afforded us the opportunity to "pool" our knowledge, compare notes and lend credence to the evidence offered by the shards.

This evidence, that Dugan did manufacture carnival glass for some time on its own, is indisputable; and that in close conjunction with Northwood Company in Wheeling, produced (on a subcontract basis) carnival glass for the Northwood concern, is also evident.

I personally examined some 40-50 shards and have identified the following patterns from the Dugan dump site:

S-Repeat	Vineyard
Nautilis	Quill
Jeweled Heart	Leaf and Beads
Maple Leaf	Windflower
Coin Spot	Apple Blossom Twigs
Pastel Swan	Garden Path
Wreath of Roses Rosebowl	Rib and Panel Vase
Apple Blossoms	Fan
Vintage Grape	Diamond and Daisy Vase
Wreathed Cherry	Woodpecker Vase
Twig Vase (Beauty Bud Vase)	Stork and Rushes
Big Basketweave	Fluted Scrolls
Rambler Rose	Grape (and Cable)
Corinth	Peacock at the Fountain
Heavy Iris	Fanciful
Holly and Berry (handled sauce)	

As the reader can readily see, at least 26 of the above patterns are not trade-marked and **could** be Dugan patterns. Both Wreathed Cherry and Fan are patterns found with the Diamond trade-mark and are definitely Dugan items.

One other point of interest is that in addition to Fanciful and Apple Blossom Twigs, it appears the Roundup pattern most people credit to the Fenton Company is also a Dugan-Northwood product since it has the same basketweave exterior as the other two patterns.

Of course the reader will have to decide for himself, the extent of Dugan's carnival glass production, but I'm convinced it was far greater than previously believed and only future research will clarify this exciting question.

I will be eternally grateful to Bill Heacock for sharing this information and personally consider it one of the major breakthroughs in carnival glass research in the last ten years.

In addition to the Dugan revelations, we've recently discovered that the Prisms pattern long attributed to the Millersburg Glass Company, has the same base and bowl exterior pattern as the Northwood Cherry and Cable covered butter so we are including it here as a possible unmarked Northwood product.

These exciting discoveries are sheer delight to the research writer and are what pushes us on.

PART ONE

All the patterns in this section (some eighty in all) are trade-marked Northwood patterns.

This merely means while they may have been manufactured at any of the plant sites connected with Harry Northwood's operations, they *are Northwood.*

In general, they represent a distinguished contribution to the world of glass, by one of its most respected members.

ACORN BURRS

Other than the famous Northwood Grape and their Peacock at Fountain pattern, Acorn Burrs is probably the most representative of the factory's work and one eagerly sought by Carnival Glass collectors.

The pattern background is that of finely done oak bark while the leaves are those of the chestnut oak. The mold-work is well done and the coloring ranks with the best.

Acorn Burrs is found in a wide range of colors and patterns and always brings top dollar.

ADVERTISING ITEMS

These come in dozens of varieties, several shapes and colors, and it would be impossible in our limited space to show them all.

Advertising items were a much welcomed area of business by *all* carnival glass makers because they were a guaranteed source of income without the usual cost-lost factor of unsold stock.

Also they could often be made with less care since they were to be given away; old molds could often be utilized, avoiding expensive new molds.

Many Northwood advertising items were small plates, with simple floral designs.

AMARYLLIS

This unusual compote is a treasure for several reasons.

First is the size (2¼" tall, 5¼" wide).

The shape is roughly triangular, rising from a slightly domed base.

The underside carries the Poppy Wreath pattern and the only colors reported are a deep purple, cobalt blue and marigold.

Amaryllis is a rather scarce pattern and isn't often mentioned in carnival glass discussions. It is, however, a unique and interesting addition to any collection.

BASKET

Novelty items are a very important area of glass production and this little item is one of the best known.

Standing on four sturdy feet, the Northwood Basket is about 5¾'' tall and 5'' across. Often the basket is simply round but sometimes one finds an example that has been pulled into a six-sided shape.

Made in a wide range of colors, including marigold, purple, cobalt, ice green, ice blue, aqua and white, this is a popular pattern.

BASKETWEAVE

Basketweave is usually an exterior pattern found on bowls and plates such as Northwood's Strawberry pattern, but I'm pleased to show the compote with a plain interior making Basketweave a primary pattern in this instance.

The coloring is excellent and is found in purple, green, marigold and possibly the pastel shades.

I couldn't resist including the second photo, showing the exterior of a small bowl. Please note the original Department Store Sticker. The price is 10 cents (marked down to 8 cents!!). How many do you want, folks?

BEADED SHELL

Known also in custard glass, Beaded Shell is one of the older patterns and is found in a variety of shapes, including berry sets, table sets, water sets and mugs.

Colors are purple, blue, green, marigold and white with blue and purple somewhat more easily found.

Beaded Shell is not marked and may be a Dugan pattern.

BEADS

It's really a shame this pattern isn't found more often and is restricted to the exterior of average size bowls, because it is a well-balanced, attractive item, especially on vivid colors.

Combining three motifs-daisy-like flowers, petalish blooms and beads - this pattern, while not rare, is certainly not plentiful and is a desirable Northwood item.

BEADED CABLE

The Beaded Cable rosebowl has long been a favorite with collectors for it is a simple yet strong design, made with all the famous Northwood quality.

Usually about 4" tall, these rosebowls stand on three sturdy legs.

The prominent cable intertwines around the middle and is, of course, edged by beads.

Nearly all pieces are marked and are made in a wide variety of colors.

Of course, these pieces are sometimes opened out to become a candy dish, like many Northwood footed items.

BLACKBERRY

While several companies had a try at a Blackberry pattern, Northwood's is one of the better ones and quite distinctive.

The pattern covers most of the allowed space, be it the interior of a 6'' compote or an 8½'' footed bowl. Combined with the latter is often a pattern called Daisy and Plume.

The colors are marigold, purple, green and white.

BLOSSOMTIME

Even if this outstanding compote were not marked, we'd surely assign it to the Northwood company because it is so typical of their work.

The flowers, the thorny branches (twisted into a geometrical overlapping star) and the curling little branchlets are all nicely done and are stippled, except for the branchlets. The background is plain and contrasts nicely.

Blossomtime is combined with an exterior pattern called Wild Flower and is found in marigold, purple, green and pastels.

The stem is quite unusual, being twisted with a screw-like pattern.

Blossomtime is a scarce pattern and always brings top dollar.

BULLS EYE AND BEADS

There are several variations of this vase pattern, often caused by the "pulling" or "slinging" to obtain height.

Nevertheless, the obvious rows of bull-eyes on the upper edge serve to establish identity.

Found mostly in Marigold, these vases are not easily found.

BULLS EYE AND LEAVES

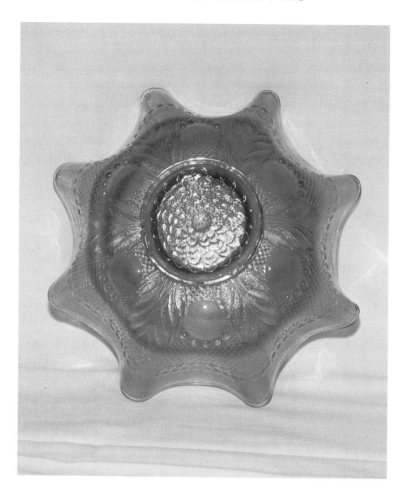

Confined to the exterior of bowls and found mostly in green or marigold, this pattern is a trifle too busy to be very effective and is certainly not one of Northwood's better efforts.

All in all, there are five motifs, including leaves, beads, circles, fishnet and a petal grouping and, although each appears on other Northwood products, not in this combination.

BUTTERFLY

The only shape chosen for this pattern is the bon-bon and most of the ones I've seen are on amethyst base glass, although marigold and green are found occasionally and pastels have been reported.

The pattern shows a lone butterfly in the center of a stippled rays pattern. Not too imaginative but the butterfly shows quite good detail.

CHERRY

Almost every carnival glass company produced one or more cherry patterns and for many years the Northwood Cherry was much confused with the Millersburg Cherry pattern.

Of course, there is a considerable difference on comparison and much of the confusion has now been dispelled.

The Northwood version is confined to bowls, flat or footed. It has fewer cherries on the branches, no stippling on the branches, and less detailed veining on the leaves.

The exterior pattern (if there is one) is often Jeweled Heart.

CHERRY AND CABLE

Sometimes called "Cherry and Thumbprint", this is a very difficult Northwood product to locate and to date I've seen one tumbler, one pitcher, a table set and a small berry bowl.

The pattern is very much a typical Northwood design and reminds one of the famous Northwood Peach, especially in the shape of the butter dish bottom which carries the same exterior base pattern as the Prisms compote.

I know of no colors except a good rich marigold, but others may certainly exist.

CORN VASE

This is one of the better known Northwood patterns and that's little wonder because it is such a good one.

Usually about 7'' tall, there are certain varients known; especially noteworthy is the rare "pulled husk" varient that was made in very limited amounts.

The colors are marigold, green, purple, ice blue, ice green and white.

The mold-work is outstanding, the color superior and the glass fine quality-truly a regal vase.

DAISY AND PLUME

Daisy and Plume is an exterior pattern found on the Northwood Blackberry large compotes as well as the primary pattern of its own compotes and footed rosebowls.

It is, of course, a very adaptable pattern and could be used on many shapes. One wonders why it does not appear on table sets or water sets, but unfortunately this is the case.

The colors are marigold, white, purple, electric blue, green and peach.

DAHLIA

Make no mistake, Dahlia is an important, often scarce, always expensive, Northwood pattern.

The glass is fine quality, the design highly raised and distinct, and the iridescence super.

Found only in marigold, purple and white, Dahlia is made only in berry sets, table sets and water sets, all useful shapes, which probably explains the scarcity due to breakage in use. The water sets are much sought.

DANDELION

I have serious misgivings about labeling *both* of the pictured items as the same pattern, but since this is how they are best known, I will yield to tradition.

Actually, the mug is certainly a dandelion pattern that is quite rare and popular, especially in aqua opalescent. Occasionally a mug bears advertising on the base and is called the "Knight Templer" mug; it brings *top* dollar!

The water set, while known as Dandelion, is *not* the same design, but nonetheless is an important Northwood pattern.

It is found in marigold, purple, green, ice blue, white, and a very rare ice green. The tankard pitcher is regal.

DIAMOND POINT

    While this is a pattern quite typical of most vase patterns, it has a certain distinction of its own. While refraining from busyness, it manages an interesting overall pattern.

    It is found in purple, blue, green, marigold, peach and white, and is normally of standard height, being 10'' - 11'' tall.

DRAPERY

This is a very graceful pattern, especially when the vase has been pulled out and down to form a lovely candy dish.

One is instantly reminded of great folds of soft satin draperies in a theater, especially in the vase shape, most of which are 10'' - 11'' in height.

The colors are marigold, peach, blue, purple, green, ice blue and ice green.

EMBROIDERED MUMS

Embroidered Mums is a rather busy pattern, saved from being overdone by a balancing of its parts.

A close cousin to the Hearts and Flowers pattern, Embroidered Mums is found on bowls and bon-bons on a stem.

Many of the pieces in this pattern carry the Thin Rib as a secondary pattern and perhaps a plate will someday be found. At least, it gives us something to hope for, because many Northwood patterns with this exterior *are* found in plates.

ENAMELED CARNIVAL GLASS

Toward the latter years of the Carnival glass "craze", patterns become simpler and in order to give the customer something different, items (especially water sets and bowls) were marketed with hand-painted enamel work on them.

Most of these were simple floral sprays, but occasionally an interesting fruit pattern emerged, like the scarce water set shown here.

Today, these seem to be gaining in popularity and certainly deserve a place in Carnival glass history.

FARMYARD

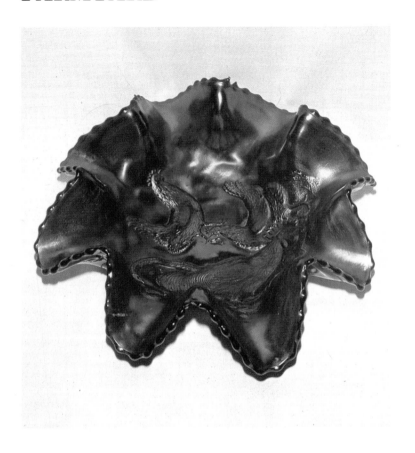

Many collectors consider this Harry Northwood's masterpiece
and it is certainly easy to see why. Massive, excellently detailed and
richly iridized, the Farmyard bowl doesn't take a backseat to any
pattern.

The shapes vary greatly and include fluted, candy-ribbon edge
and even a square shape.

Found mostly in purple or fiery amethyst, a single green bowl
and a peach opalescent one are know and have commanded the
prices only great rarities are capable of bringing.

FEATHERS

Northwood certainly made its share of vases-perhaps because they were so decorative and useful.

The Feathers vase is an average example usually found in marigold, purple and green and is of average size and quality.

FERN

Again we find a pattern that is sometimes combined with the well-known Northwood pattern, Daisy and Plume.

Fern is usually found as an interior pattern on bowls and compotes.

It is an attractive pattern but really not an outstanding one.

FINE CUT AND ROSES

The real pleasure of this pattern is the successful combination of a realistic floral pattern with a pleasing geometric one.

Of course rosebowls have a charm all their own.

Really well done mold-work and super color all add to its attraction and even though it is slightly smaller than many rosebowl patterns, it is a favorite of collectors.

FINE RIB

Can you imagine anything simpler? Yet the Fine Rib pattern was and is a success to the extent it was used time and time again by the Northwood company as secondary patterns and is the primary one in attractive vases like the one shown.

While common in marigold and purple, the green color is a scarce one in Fine Rib.

FLUTE

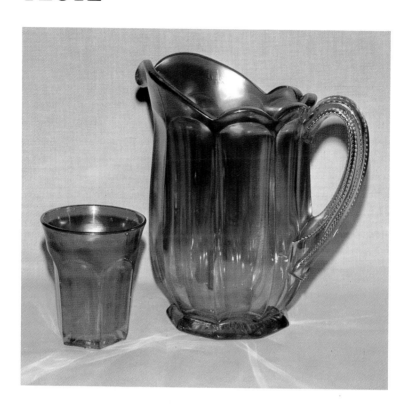

While it is certainly true all of the major makers of carnival glass used the Flute pattern in one way or another, apparently only Imperial and Northwood thought enough of it to make it a primary pattern.

Thus we find many useful shapes in an array of colors coming from the Northwood factories-including sherbets, water sets, table sets, berry sets and even individual salt dips (an item seldom encountered in carnival glass).

The green water set is probably the rarest color and shape in this pattern.

FRUIT AND FLOWERS

Apparantly a very close relative to the Three Fruits pattern, this is another of Northwood floral groupings so well designed and produced.

Also there are several variations of this pattern, some with more flowers intermingled with the apples, pears and cherries, often meandering almost to the very outer edge of the glass.

Again the Northwood Basketweave is the exterior pattern and Fruits and Flowers is found on compotes with handles as well as bowls.

GRACEFUL

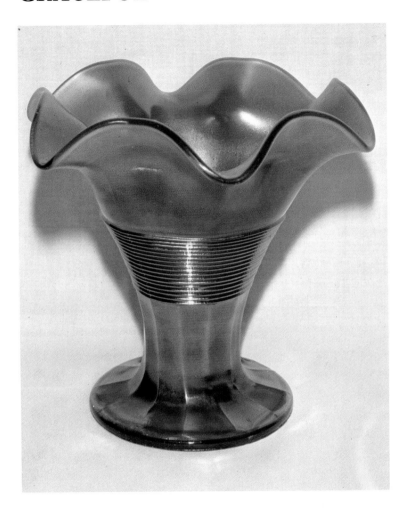

Once again we find a very simple pattern, so very different from most Northwood offerings in the carnival glass field.

Found mostly on marigold, occasionally a rich purple or deep emerald green vase in this pattern will surface and when one of these is found, the simple beauty of the Graceful pattern becomes obvious.

GRAPE (AND CABLE)

Northwood Grape is, without question, the all-time favorite in carnival glass. Not only did it lead the field sixty years ago, but it still does.

The variety of shapes available is staggering and the color availability large; the pastels are especially sought.

Of course this pattern usually brings top dollar, especially in the rare shapes and colors. A small spittoon recently sold for $7000.00 at the Wishard auction.

Whatever the undeniable appeal, this uncomplicated pattern has to be rated as the top item and entire collections of Grape aren't uncommon.

GRAPE AND GOTHIC ARCHES

Made in a variety of kinds of glass, including crystal, custard, gold decorated, and carnival glass, this patern is certainly one of the earlier grape patterns.

The arches are very effective, reminding one of a lacy arbor framing the grapes and leaves.

While the berry sets often go unnoticed, the water sets are very desirable and are a must for all Northwood collectors.

GRAPE ARBOR

Here is another underated pattern, especially in the large footed bowl shape which carries the same exterior pattern as the Butterfly and Tulip pattern.

Of course the tankard water set is popular, especially in the pastel colors of ice blue, ice green and white. The marigold set seldom brings top dollar and this is a shame for it is quite nice.

The only other shape in Grape Arbor is a quite scarce hat shape. While it is found in cobalt blue, this color has never surfaced in the water set, a rather unusual situation.

GRAPE LEAVES

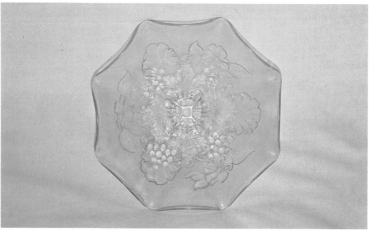

Harry Northwood must have loved this pattern, for I've never seen a poor example. The purple bowls are, almost without exception, vividly brilliant with strong color and iridescence.

And the ice blue, shown here, is one of the prettiest items in this color I've ever seen.

It is sad no other shape was chosen for the Grape Leaves pattern, but this is the case.

The exterior is the familiar Wild Rose pattern with a finely stippled background.

GREEK KEY

This simple continuous pattern, called Roman Key in pressed glass, is really very attractive when iridized.

Actually, there are three motifs used; the Ray central pattern, the Greek Key and the Beads (in the much sought water set a fourth motif of prisms is added).

Besides the water set there are flat and footed bowls as well as plates. The colors are both vivid and pastels.

HEARTS AND FLOWERS

Hearts and Flowers is an intricate pattern, like so many others favored by the Northwood company. It is found on various sizes and shapes of bowls as well as small, very graceful compotes.

Apparently it was designed as a close relative of the Fanciful and Embroidered Mums patterns, perhaps by the same mold-maker.

Interestingly enough, the compotes in the pattern are very similar in shape to the Persian Medallion compotes attributed to the Fenton Glass Company.

HOLIDAY

Without a doubt, this is a most puzzling pattern on a shape that is unique in Carnival Glass.

This 11'' tray is on heavy glass. The pattern is all exterior and moderately raised, including the trademark.

The color is deep marigold.

Just what this particular tray's use was is not known as no other shapes with this pattern have been reported. A change tray, perhaps? A lemonade tray? Someday, we may know but until then, we'll just have to admire the attractive design and speculate.

JEWELED HEART

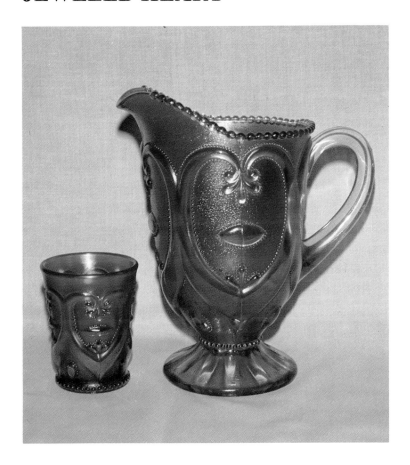

Carried over from the pressed glass era, Jeweled Heart is, of course, the famous exterior pattern of the Farmyard bowl. However, it is used as a primary pattern on very scarce water sets when the pitcher is footed - a not common shape for water pitchers in Carnival glass.

I have seen Jeweled Heart in purple, peach and marigold only but other colors may exist. If so, they would be considered ultra-rare.

JOCKEY CLUB

Although very much akin to the Good Luck pattern, Jockey Club is certainly a separate pattern and a quick once-over will establish this fact. The floral arrangements are entirely different, even the horse-shoe and riding crop are not the same.

Jockey club is found on trade-marked bowls which carry the Northwood Basketweave as an exterior pattern. The ones I'm familiar with have been on a good amethyst glass, well iridized.

LEAF AND BEADS

Here is another very well-known Northwood pattern found not only in Carnival Glass but clear and opalescent glass as well.

Available on bowls as well as rose bowls, the twig feet are used by more than one Carnival Glass maker. However, the trade-mark is usually present.

Leaf and Beads is found in a wide range of colors including marigold, green, purple, ice green, ice blue and white.

LEAF COLUMN

While not a spectacular pattern, here is a vase that takes on new importance on second glance. It is a well-balanced all-over pattern that does the job nicely.

The iridescence, especially on the dark colors, is quite nice. The shape is attractive and the vase is, of course, a very useful item.

Certainly any collection of Carnival glass would benefit by adding one of these.

LOVELY

Northwood's Lovely is a seldom seen interior pattern found on footed bowls with Leaf and Beads as an exterior pattern.

While we can't be certain, it is possible this motif was added at the Dugan factory since shards of Leaf and Beads were found there.

The colors seen thus far are marigold and purple with very good iridescence.

LUSTRE FLUTE

Again we have a very familiar pattern to most collectors, but one that is not really too distinguished.

I suppose not every pattern should be expected to be spectacular.

The shape I've seen most often is the hat shape in both green and marigold, but punch sets, berry sets, breakfast sets, bon-bons, nappies and compotes do exist in marigold, green and purple.

The base is many-rayed and usually the Northwood trademark is present.

MANY FRUITS

This is a truly lovely fruit pattern, something that any company would be proud to claim.

The mold work is heavy and distinct, the design is interesting and quite realistic and the coloration flawless.

I personally prefer the ruffled base, but that is a small matter.

Many Fruits would have made a beautiful water set.

The colors are marigold, blue, white, purple and green.

MAPLE LEAF

Maple Leaf is a carry-over pattern from the custard glass line, but in carnival glass is limited to stemmed berry sets, table sets and water sets.

I examined shards of this pattern from the Dugan dump site, so items in carnival glass were obviously turned out at that factory, probably for the Northwood Company.

At any rate, the background is the same Soda Gold pattern as that found on the exterior of Garden Path bowls and plates.

Maple Leaf was made in marigold, purple, cobalt blue and green.

MEMPHIS

While an interesting geometrical pattern, Memphis has never been one of my favorites-possibly because of its limited shapes. I can imagine how much my interest would increase if a water set were to appear!

I have seen an enormous banquet punch set in crystal, but the size was not made in carnival glass.

The shapes are a berry set, punch set, fruit bowl on separate stand, and a compote.

The colors found are both vivid and pastel with the ice blue shown being a real beauty.

NAUTILIS

It is certainly a shame Harry Northwood did not carry over more shapes of this pattern into carnival glass because every piece of the custard shapes are a joy.

In Carnival we find only the small novelty piece described as a boat shape (actually one large footed berry bowl has been seen in marigold - a very, very rare piece of carnival glass!)

It appears with either both ends turned up or one end turned down and the colors are peach and purple.

Some of the Nautilis pieces are signed on the bottom in script and are more valuable than unsigned ones.

NEAR-CUT

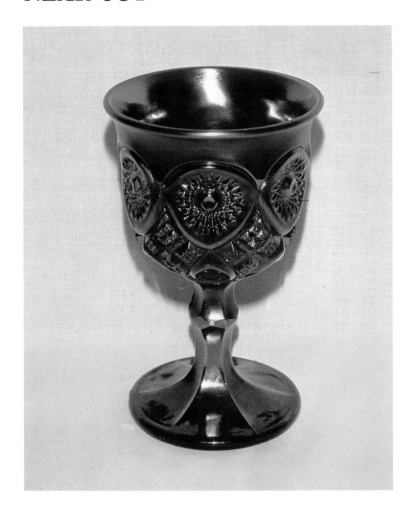

This attractive pattern is quite similar to the Hobstar Flower shown elsewhere in this book.

In addition to the compote and goblet, made from the same mold, there is a very rare water pitcher. I have heard of no tumblers but they may exist.

The colors are marigold and purple with the latter most seen.

NIPPON

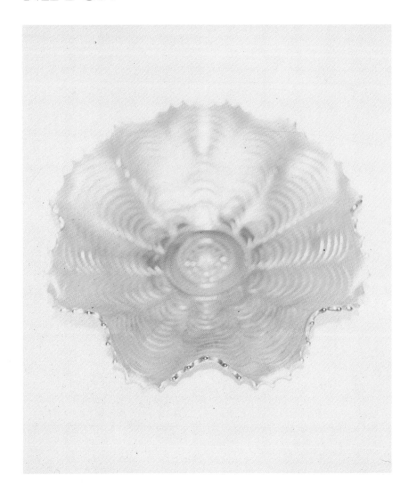

Certainly Nippon must have been a popular pattern in its heyday, for it is readily found today.

The pattern is simple but effective; a central stylized blossom with panels of drapery extending toward the outer edges of the bowl.

Found in a wide variety of colors, including marigold, green, purple, ice green and white, Nippon is a nice pattern to own.

OCTET

Even if this pattern were not marked, we would attribute it to the Northwood Company because the exterior pattern is the Northwood vintage found on the Star of David and Bows bowl.

Octet is also a dome-footed bowl, usually about 8½" in diameter.

It is a simple, but effective, pattern-one that wouldn't be easily confused with others.

The colors are marigold, purple, green and pastels of white and ice green. The purple is most often found.

ORIENTAL POPPY

Here is a very impressive, realistic pattern, especially effective on the chosen shape - a tankard water set.

The mold work is clear and clean and the glass is quality all the way.

Colors are marigold, green, purple, white, ice green and ice blue.

PANELLED HOLLY

Panelled Holly is found in crystal, gilt glass and carnival glass. However, the range of shapes is much less in the latter, limited to the exteriors of bowls, footed bon-bons, and an extremely rare water pitcher.

While fairly attractive, Panelled Holly is really not a great pattern. It appears a trifle busy, a bit confused.

The most often seen color is green, however purple and marigold do exist and I've seen a combination of green glass with marigold iridescence.

PEACH

Once more we show a Northwood pattern that was also produced in other types of glass. This was more-than-likely one of the earlier Northwood Carnival glass patterns and is found in a very fine cobalt blue as well as white, the latter often with gilting.

What a shame more shapes were not made in peach, for only berry sets, table sets and water sets are known.

The pattern is scarce and always brings top dollar.

PEACOCKS

Often called "Peacocks on the Fence", this Northwood pattern typifies what Carnival glass is really all about.

An interesting pattern, well molded, and turned out in a variety of appealing colors, Peacocks is a delight.

Only average size bowls and plates are known, but the color range is wide, including vivid colors, pastels and a really beautiful aqua opalescent.

The exterior usually carries a wide rib pattern.

PEACOCK AND URN

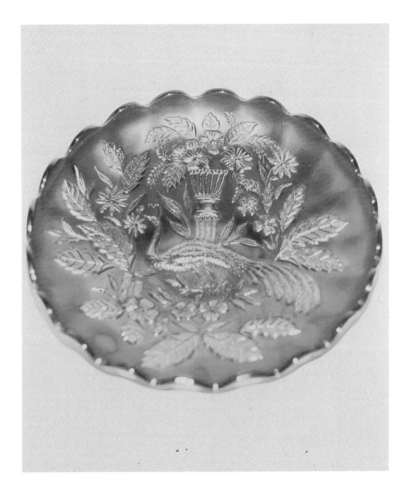

This subject must have been very appealing to the mass market for not only did Northwood have a version of Peacock and Urn but so did Fenton and, of course, Millersburg.

And while there is little chance to confuse the Fenton version with the others, the Millersburg and Northwood patterns are quite similar.

The Northwood Peacock and Urn is most often found on ice cream sets, has three rows of beading on the urns and has more *open space* between the design and the outer edges of the bowl.

Colors include both vivids and pastels as well as aqua opalescent.

PEACOCK AT THE FOUNTAIN

Peacock at the Fountain probably rates as Northwood's second most popular pattern, right on the heels of the famous Northwood Grape and its easy to see why.

It is an impressive, well done pattern with an intriguing design.

Available in berry sets, table sets, punch sets, water sets, compotes and a large footed orange bowl, Peacock at the Fountain was made in a host of colors, including the much prized ice green and aqua opalescent.

Shards of this pattern were found at Dugan, leading us to believe Harry Northwood "farmed out" work to the Dugan Glass Company to keep up with demand on his best selling patterns.

PETAL AND FAN

Found only in bowls of various sizes, this pattern also has the Jeweled Heart as an exterior design.

The motif itself is simple but attractive: a series of alternating stippled and plain petals on a plain ribbed background with a fan-like design growing from each plain petal.

The feeling is almost one of ancient Egypt where such fans were made of feathers.

Petals and Fans is available in many colors including peach opalescent.

POPPY

Poppy is most often found on small oval bowls, described as trays or, with the sides crimped, as pickle dishes. However, it is also found as an exterior pattern on larger bowls, some with plain interiors, others with a large Daisy in the center of the bowl.

The colors are electric blue, marigold, peach, purple and white. Others may exist but these are the ones I've seen.

RASPBERRY

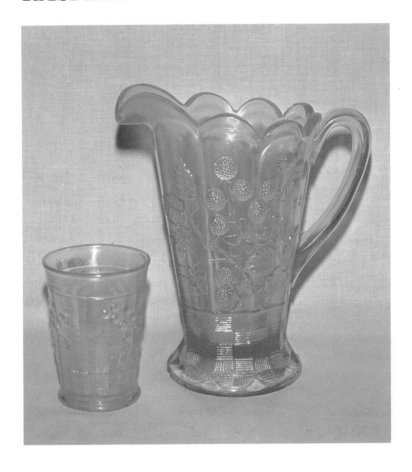

Even without the famous trademark, this pattern would be recognized as a Northwood product, for it includes the basket-weave so often found on that company's designs.

Available in water sets, table sets, berry sets and a milk pitcher, Raspberry has long been a favorite with collectors.

The colors are marigold, green, purple, ice blue and ice green with the richly lustered purple most prevalent.

ROSETTE

Combining several well-known carnival glass patterns, including Stippled Rays, Beads, and Prisms, this Northwood pattern isn't the easiest thing to find.

In arrangement, it reminds one of the Greek Key pattern, but Rosette stands on its own.

Found only on generous sized bowls, the colors are marigold and amethyst. Green may be a possibility, but I haven't seen one.

SINGING BIRDS

Found in custard glass, crystal and carnival glass, Singing Birds is one of the better-known Northwood patterns.

The shapes are berry sets, table sets, water sets and mugs in vivid and pastel colors.

An ice blue Singing Birds mug sold for an astounding $800.00 at the Wishard auction in 1977 and the same shape in aqua opalescent is even more valuable.

SPRINGTIME

In many ways this pattern is similar to Northwood's Raspberry pattern, especially since both are bordered at the bottom with versions of a basketweave.

Springtime, however, is really its own master and bears panels of wheat, flowers and butterflies above and throughout the basketweave.

Found in berry sets, table sets and very scarce water sets in marigold, green, amethyst and also in pastels, Springtime is a very desirable pattern.

STAR OF DAVID AND BOWS

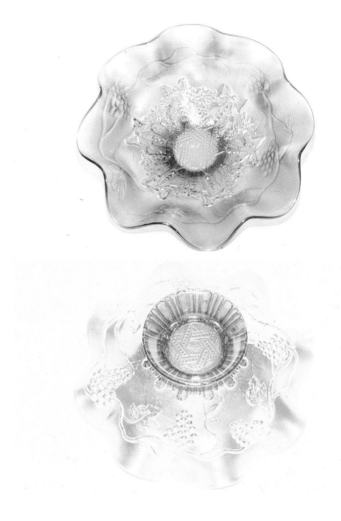

The Northwood version of this figure (Imperial also produced a Star of David bowl) is a very attractive dome footed bowl and is a tribute to the Jewish religion.

The Star is interlaced and is beaded while a graceful border of flowers, tendrils and bows edge the stippled center.

The exterior is the Vintage pattern and the colors are marigold, green and amethyst.

STIPPLED RAYS (AND VARIENTS)

Every carnival-producing glass company had a stippled rays pattern and it is probably the most common motif in the entire field of iridized glass other than the grape.

Northwood had several versions. The one shown is a varient. The most unusual aspects of the bowl are the *reversed* N and the exterior pattern which is a Greek Key and Scales pattern.

As you can see, it is a beautiful fiery amethyst and the bowl is dome footed.

Stippled Rays was made in most colors and several shapes.

STRAWBERRY

Available in only bowls of various sizes and plates in either flat or hand grip styles, this well-known Northwood pattern comes either plain or stippled. On the stippled version, there are three narrow rings around the outer edge; these are absent on the plain pieces.

Colors are both vivid and pastel with the purple showing off the pattern to its best.

STRAWBERRY INTAGLIO

I showed this pattern in my first glass book as a questionable Millersburg pattern. Since then we've been able to trace it to the Northwood Company through both a "goofus" bowl and a gilt decorated one, both bearing the famous trade-mark.

The glass is *thick*, the design deeply impressed and the irridescence only so-so. I've seen large and small bowls only.

SUNFLOWER

Sunflower must have been a very popular pattern in its day, for numerous examples have survived to the present time.

It's quite easy to see why it was in demand. It's a pretty, well designed pattern that holds iridescence beautifully.

The bowl is footed and carries the very pleasing Meander pattern on the exterior.

It is also found, rarely, on a plate. The colors are marigold, green and amethyst.

SWIRL

I've seen this pattern on a beautiful tankard water set and the mug shape in marigold only, although the tumbler is shown in the Owens book in green and is known in amethyst. And while the tumblers are often marked, the mug isn't.

Now and then the tankard pitcher is found with enameled flowers added. Naturally the pitcher is scarce and the mug is considered rare. Candlesticks also exist.

THREE FRUITS

So very close in design to the Northwood Fruits and Flowers pattern shown earlier in this book, the two substantial differences are the absence of the small flowers and the addition of an extra cluster of cherries to this pattern.

Found in bowls of all sizes, including flat and footed ones, and average size plates. Three Fruits is available in all vivid colors as well as pastels.

TORNADO

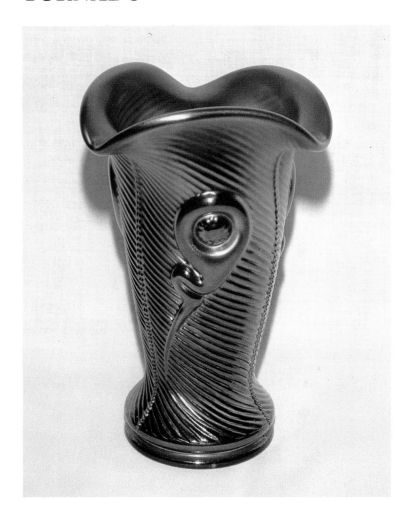

Perhaps because it is one of the most unusual vases in all of carnival glass, Tornado is always a favorite with collectors.

Available in both plain and ribbed, the size may vary considerably and I've seen a mini-version in marigold.

The colors are marigold, green, purple, white and ice blue. The Northwood trade-mark is found on the inside of the vase.

TOWN PUMP

Certainly there isn't one collector of carnival glass who isn't familiar with this very famous pattern.

The Town Pump is almost 7" tall and is mostly on purple, although marigold and green are found in limited quantities.

The design is simple but very pleasing - ivy twining over a stippled background with a crude tree bark spout and handle.

No carnival glass collection would be complete without this pattern and certainly it deserves a prominent place in any Northwood collection.

TREE TRUNK

Simple but effective is the bark-like pattern for this popular vase. Apparently it was a well-liked pattern when it was being manufactured for many examples exist in sizes from 8'' to tall 20'' ones.

The colors are marigold, blue, purple, green and white.

TWO FRUITS

    Here is a Northwood trade-marked pattern so unique and so very rare, it is not listed in the two major pattern guides.

    Shown is the spooner in a rich cobalt blue. It last sold in the 1977 Wishard auction. I know of one other piece in this pattern, a lidless sugar.

    Shown is the cherry side; the other pattern on the opposite side shows two peaches.

    The spooner measures 6¼" x 4½" and bears the Northwood trademark.

WATERLILY AND CATTAILS

Here is a pattern used in different degrees by both the North-wood and Fenton Companies and at times it's rather hard to tell who made what.

The obvious Fenton rendition is the exterior pattern used on the Thistle banana boat, but it is believed they made other shapes in Water Lily and Cattails, including a whimsey toothpick.

The Northwood shapes are berry sets, table sets and water sets. All are available in marigold and the berry sets and water sets are occasionally found in blue.

WHEAT

Make no mistake about it, this is a *very rare* pattern, known in only a covered sweetmeat (2 known) and a single bowl in colors of green and amethyst.

Surfacing in carnival glass circles only in the last couple of years, these rarities have caused much excitement and brought astonishing prices where they've been shown.

The sweetmeat is the same shape as the Northwood Grape pattern.

What a pity we don't have more of this truly important pattern.

WILD ROSE

This well-known Northwood pattern is used on the exterior of two types of bowls. The first is an average flat bowl, often with no interior pattern. The second, however, is an unusual footed bowl, rather small, with an edge of open work in fan-like figures. Certainly, the intricacy of this open work took much care and skill.

The colors are marigold, amethyst, green and occasionally pastels.

WILD STRAWBERRY

One might think of this as the "grown-up" version of the regular Northwood Strawberry since it is much the same.

The primary difference is the addition of the blossoms to the patterning and, of course, the size of the bowl itself; which is about 1½" larger in diameter.

I have seen two exterior designs used. The most common by far is the standard basketweave, while rarely we encounter the Jeweled Heart pattern. This latter pattern really adds a good deal of class to the whole.

The colors are rich, vivid greens and purples.

WISHBONE

I personally feel this is one of the most graceful patterns in carnival glass. The lines just flow, covering much of the allowed space.

Found on water sets, which are very scarce, flat and footed bowls, plates and a very stately one-lily epergne, Wishbone is usually accompanied by the basketweave pattern on the exterior.

My favorite color is the ice blue, but Wishbone is available in marigold, green, purple, blue, white and ice green.

WISTERIA

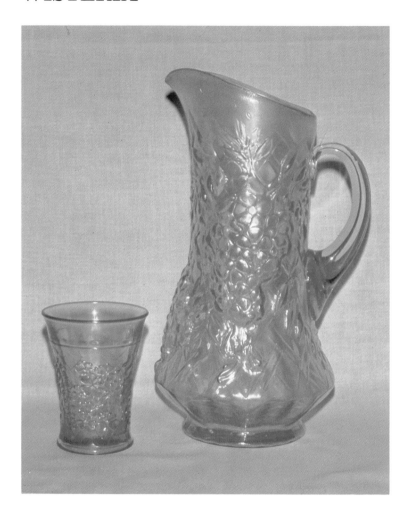

What a beautiful pattern this is! Certainly a first cousin to the Grape Arbor pattern in iridescent glass as well as the Lattice and Cherry pattern in crystal, Wisteria is unfortunately found only on water sets.

While only tumblers in ice green have surfaced, both pitchers and tumblers are known in white and a really outstanding ice blue.

What a shame no vivid colors are available in this Northwood masterpiece.

PART TWO

Here we have chosen to show all the questionable patterns, forty-odd in all, none marked, but certainly all *possible* contenders for membership in the Northwood family.

Included are the twenty-odd patterns of glass for which shards were found in the Dugan dump site in Indiana, Pennsylvania, as well as patterns many collectors have long felt might be Northwood products.

Any speculation on my part is just *that* and will be proven or disproven with time. As all of you know, I am not infallible.

APPLE BLOSSOMS

Found only in smallish bowls or plates, Apple Blossoms seem to be a very average carnival glass pattern, produced for a mass market in large quantities.

Most often seen in Marigold, it is occasionally found in vivid colors as well as pastels, especially white.

A quarter size chunk of this pattern in white was found at the Dugan dump site in 1975.

APPLE BLOSSOM TWIGS

This is a very popular pattern, especially in plates where the design is shown to full advantage.

The detail is quite nice with fine mold work, much like that of Acorn Burrs.

Found mostly in marigold, peach and purple, Apple Blossom Twigs has as its exterior pattern, the Big Basketweave pattern.

Shards in this pattern at the Dugan site have been identified.

BEAUTY BUD VASE (TWIGS)

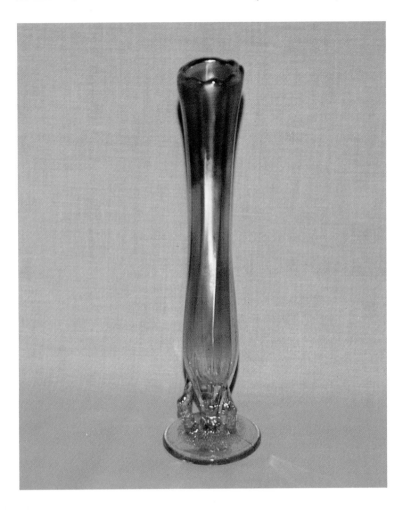

The most distinctive feature is of course the twig-like feet, intended to be tree roots and these vases are found in sizes from 3½" to 11" tall.

Marigold is the most plentiful color and often only the top shows any hues at all, but the tiny purple version is a beauty and is much sought by vase collectors.

BIG BASKETWEAVE

Found primarily as a vase pattern, this is also the exterior pattern of Fanciful, Apple Blossom Twigs and Round-up patterns.

It is found in most colors, including marigold, peach, cobalt, purple, green and white.

The vases range in size from 9'' to 11'' and are especially nice in the darker colors.

BUTTERFLY AND TULIP

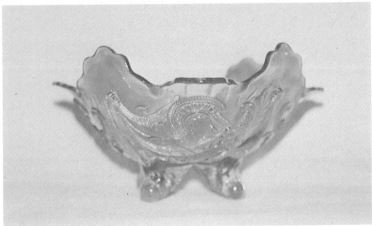

Make no mistake about it, this is a very impressive pattern. The bowl is large, the glass heavy and the mold work exceptional.

Found in either marigold or purple, this footed jewel has the famous Feather Scroll for an exterior pattern.

Typically, the shallower the bowl, the more money it brings, with the purple bringing many times the price of the *underated* marigold.

COIN SPOT

This undistinguished little compote holds a dear spot in my heart for it was the first piece of carnival glass we ever owned.

Made in opalescent glass also, in carnival glass it is found in marigold, green, purple, peach and white.

The design is simple, consisting of alternate rows of indented stippled ovals and plain flat panels.

The stem is rather ornate with a finial placed mid-way down.

Often in marigold, the stem remains clear glass.

DAISY AND DRAPE

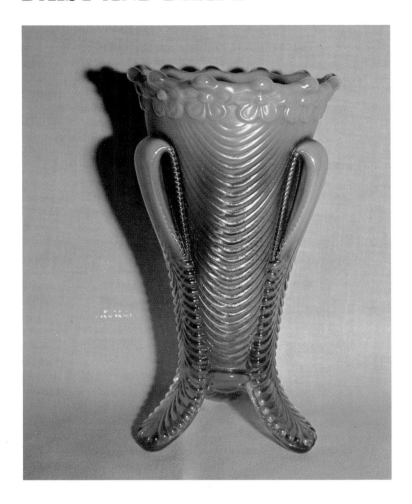

This pattern is probably a spin-off of the old U.S. Glass pattern, "Vermont", the main difference being the standing row of daisies around the top edge.

Made in most of the Northwood colors, the purple leads the vivid colors, while aqua opalescent is the most sought of the pastels. White is probably the most available color, but even it brings top dollar.

DOGWOOD SPRAYS

This is a pattern so very familiar to all carnival collectors, for there are probably more bowls with various floral sprays than any other design.

Dogwood Sprays, while well done, is not extraordinary in any sense of the word.

Found on both bowls and compotes, the color most seen is peach, but purple does turn up from time to time.

The bowl, like so many Northwood bowls, is dome footed.

FANCIFUL

Probably many collectors will challenge this pattern appearing in a Northwood book, but shards from the Dugan factory were identified by this author in both marigold and purple, so here it is.

Actually, if a comparison is carefully made with the Embroidered Mums, Heart and Flowers and Fancy patterns, one finds a close similarity that isn't evident on first glance.

Fanciful is available on bowls and plates in colors of marigold, peach, purple and white. The familiar Big Basketweave adorns the exterior.

FAN

Despite the fact most collectors have credited this pattern to Northwood, I'm really convinced it was a Dugan product. In custard glass it has been found with the well-known Diamond marking.

Of course many more shapes of the Fan pattern were made in custard. In carnival glass, the availability is limited to the sauce dish and an occasional piece that is footed and has a handle.

The colors seen are marigold, peach, and purple. Peach is the most available color.

FIVE HEARTS

Like so many of the Northwood patterns in peach opalescent, Five Hearts is found only on dome footed bowls of average size.

It has been estimated that some sixty to seventy-five percent of all peach carnival was made by this company; personally, I'd say it would be closer to ninety percent. Certainly Harry Northwood must have felt it was an exciting inovation in the glass field.

GARDEN PATH

Both the regular Garden Path and the varient will surprise many people appearing here but apparently they are either Northwood or Dugan patterns since I have catalogued a large chunk of a peach bowl from the Dugan diggings.

The exterior pattern is Soda Gold, a pattern long believed to be an Imperial Glass pattern, but again let us emphasize "if it comes in peach carnival, it is probably a Northwood product".

The 11" Garden Paths plate is one of the more renowned pieces of carnival glass and has sold for prices in excess of $4000.00.

GOOD LUCK

I'm sure every carnival glass collector is familiar with this pattern since most of us have found a place for an example in our collections at one time or another.

The example shown is quite unusual in that it is a true aqua blue with reddish iridescence. It is the only example I've ever seen in this exact color although the Good Luck bowls and plates are found in a very wide range of colors.

While some writers have attributed this pattern to both Fenton and Northwood, I seriously doubt if the Fenton Company ever produced this pattern.

GRAPE DELIGHT

Here is a pattern I'm sure will bring on a few outcries, because I've often heard it declared to be a Fenton product, but I'm very sure it came from the Northwood family.

On close comparison with several Northwood products, the mold-work is certainly compatible.

Not only does it come in the scarce nut bowl shape shown but in the more often seen rosebowl.

The colors are both vivid and pastel and the most unusual feature, the six stubby feet.

GRAPEVINE LATTICE

I personally doubt the plate shown is really the same pattern as the water set known by the same name, but will give in to tradition and list them as one and the same.

The plate and bowl could be called "Twigs" since they closely resemble the Apple Blossom Twigs pattern minus the flowers and leaves.

The colors are both vivid and pastels, usually with very good iridescence.

HEAVY IRIS

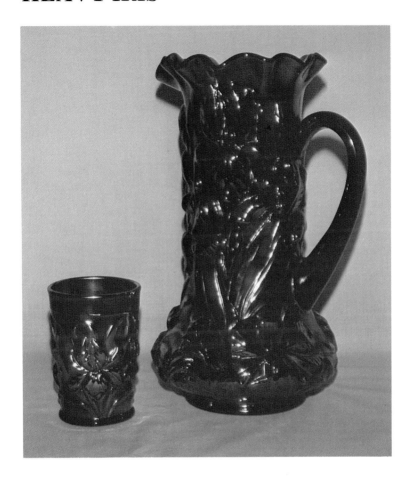

I'm sure every collector of carnival glass has speculated at one time or another over the maker of this beautiful pattern. Some have felt Millersburg, others Fenton. Now, however, it is with some assurance we report that a very sizeable chunk of a Heavy Iris tumbler was unearthed at the Dugan dump site in 1975 so we can declare it either a Dugan or Northwood pattern.

The only shape is, of course, a graceful tankard water set. The design is sharp and heavy, simple enough to be effective yet covering much of the available space.

The colors are marigold, purple and white with purple the most desired. All in all, a beautiful set to own.

HEAVY WEB

Found primarily on large, thick bowls in peach opalescent, Heavy Web is a very interesting pattern.

It has been found with two distinct exterior patterns -- a beautifully realistic grape and leaf design covering most of the surface and an equally attractive morning glory pattern.

I've seen various shapes including round, ruffled, square and elongated ones. A vivid purple or green bowl in this pattern would certainly be a treasure.

HOBSTAR FLOWER

This beautiful little compote is seldom seen and usually comes as a surprise to most collectors. I've heard it called "Octagon" or "Fashion" at one time or another, and most people say they've never seen it before.

It is a rather hard to find item and the one pictured is only the second I've run across. It has been reported in marigold, but I can't verify this.

At any rate, the design is strong, the glass good quality and the iridescence quite superior. Hobstar Flower would certainly be a credit to any collection.

HOLLY AND BERRY

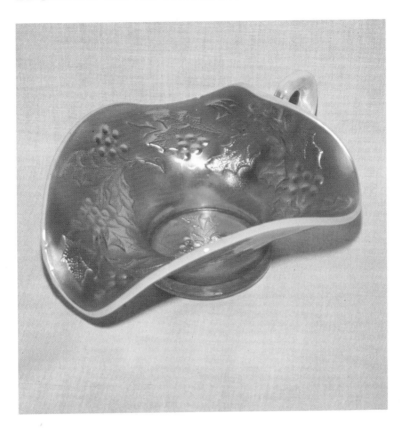

This pattern, found mostly in rather deep bowls and nappies (one-handled bon-bons) as well as an occasional sauce boat, is so similar to the Millersburg Holly pattern, most people simply accept it as a product of that Company.

The one distinguishing difference is the leaf and berry medallion in the center of the Holly and Berry pattern while the Millersburg design has no such center motif.

Holly and Berry is found in purple, green, marigold, blue and most often peach opalescent.

A large piece of this pattern was discovered in the Dugan diggings.

IDYLL*

When the Battins brought this vase for me to photograph, I was highly impressed with it.

Obviously, it is a rare, little-known pattern, but beyond that, it is an intersting design, well executed and ever-so-typical of North wood's genuis.

The water-lillies, the hovering butterflies, the graceful, swaying plants all blend into a picture both rewarding and distinguished.

The color is a beautiful deep amethyst, iridized both inside and out. The height is nearly 7 inchs and there are three water lily panels around the middle.

*Possibly Fenton

POINSETTIA

For some reason, in years past, someone attributed this very stylish pattern to the Fenton Glass Company. Just why, I can't guess for Poinsettia was made by Northwood in custard glass and was illustrated in their advertising of the day.

At any rate, this mistake has been corrected and we now recognize this well-done bowl as a Harry Northwood design.

Poinsettia is found either as a flat based or footed bowl with the Fine Rib as an exterior pattern. The finish is nearly always superior. The colors are marigold, green, purple, fiery amethyst, white and ice green.

POINSETTIA, INTERIOR*

Here is something unusual - a tumbler with all the pattern on the inside. Of course, we've all seen the Northwood Swirl pattern which is also an interior one, but that was a simple geometrical design while the Interior Poinsettia is an offering of a large flower.

Apparently these were never very popular for they are very scarce. Also, to the best of my knowledge, no pitcher has been found. The iridescence is on both the inside and outside and is a good rich marigold.

*Northwood? Absolutely - some are marked.

PRISMS

Those of you who have read my Millersburg book will be somewhat surprised to see this pattern shown here, but as we said in the introduction to this book, we now have evidence to support a Northwood origin for this unusual little compote.

For quite a while amethyst was the only color seen, but here is a marigold of which I've seen some four or five and I suspect green also exists.

Prisms measure 7¼" across the handles and is 2½" tall. The pattern is all exterior and is intaglio with an ornate star under the base like the one on the Cherry and Cable butterdish.

QUESTION MARKS

Here is a simple pattern found on the interiors of bon bons and occasionally compotes like the one shown.

Again the exterior is usually plain and the colors are peach opalescent, marigold, purple and white.

Both the compote and the bon bon are footed; the compote is one of the small size, measuring 4½'' tall and 4'' across the highly ruffled edge.

QUILL

Once again we show a pattern of which shards were found in the Dugan diggings and I truly believe Quill was indeed a Dugan Glass Company pattern. But since we can not rule out Northwood as the maker, we show it here.

The pitcher is some 10" tall and has a base diameter of 4½". The colors are marigold and amethyst and the iridescence is usually above average.

Quill is a scarce pattern and apparently small quantities were made, again pointing toward the Dugan Company as the manufacturer.

The water set is the only shape.

RAINDROPS

Here is another of the dome footed bowls available in peach opalescent like so many offered by the Northwood Company. Remember, I said earlier that I felt Northwood was responsible for at least 90% of the peach carnival and a close study of these bowls will support this belief.

Raindrops is found without stippling. It has the Keyhole pattern as an exterior companion and has four mold marks.

All in all, it is a nice pattern to own, especially if you like peach opalescent glass.

RAMBLER ROSE

Until quite recently, I'd always felt Rambler Rose was a Fenton product, but upon examining a large shard of this pattern from the Dugan dump site, I'm compelled to admit my mistake.

Whether made by Dugan or Northwood I'm still not sure, but it certainly isn't Fenton.

This water set has a bulbous pitcher with a ruffled top. The flowers are well designed and clearly molded.

The colors are marigold, purple, blue and green.

Perhaps research in the years ahead will add more information about this pattern.

ROSE SHOW

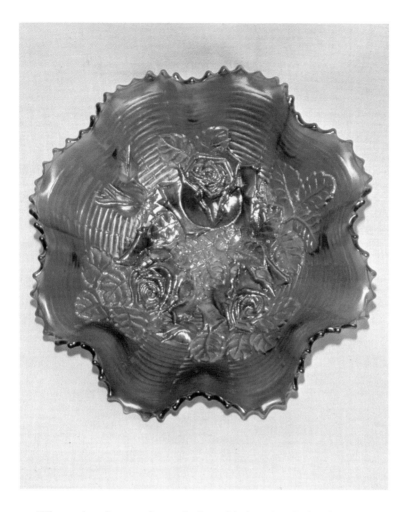

What a handsome piece of glass this is! The design is flawless, heavy and covering every inch of available space. Yet it isn't in the least bit busy-looking.

One has the distinct feeling he is looking into a reeded basket of fresh-cut roses and can almost smell the perfume.

Found only on bowls and a plate varient, the beautiful pattern was produced in small amounts in marigold, purple, blue, green, white, ice blue, ice green, peach opalescent, amber, aqua opalescent and a rare ice green opalescent.

ROUND-UP

I expect to receive a lot of argument about the Round-up pattern appearing in a Northwood book, but if we are to be completely honest, we must admit the possibility.

As I earlier stated, Round-up, Fanciful and Apple Blossom Twigs all have the *same exterior* pattern and shards of the latter two were found in the Dugan diggings.

Found only on bowls, ruffled plates and true plates, Round-up is available in marigold, purple, peach opalescent, blue, amber, white and a pale shade of lavender.

The true plate is quite scarce and always brings top dollar.

S-REPEAT

Made in crystal, decorated crystal and gilt glass prior to being made in Carnival Glass, S-Repeat is found in only a small range of shapes in iridized glass.

Besides the punch set shown, there is a rare toothpick that has been widely reproduced and a handful of marigold tumblers that some believe are questionable.

At any rate, in Carnival Glass, S-Repeat is a very scarce item.

SCALES

Most of these bowls I've seen are on the small size - 6'' - 7'' in diameter.

Nevertheless, they are well done, interesting items and add much to any collection.

The Fishscale pattern is on the interior while the Beads design is on the exterior. When held to the light, one pattern fits happily into position to compliment the whole, giving a pleasant experience.

SIX PETALS

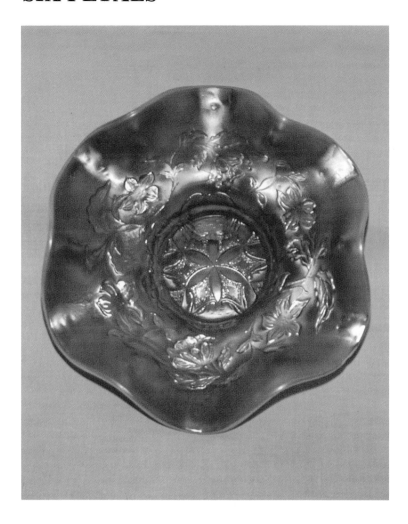

Nearly always seen in shallow bowls in peach opalescent, Six Petals is occasionally found in a rare plate.

The other colors available are purple, green, blue and white.

Possibly this was a Dugan pattern rather than a Northwood one and in many ways it reminds one of the Holly and Berry pattern shown elsewhere in the book.

The exterior is plain on the examples I've seen.

SKI STAR

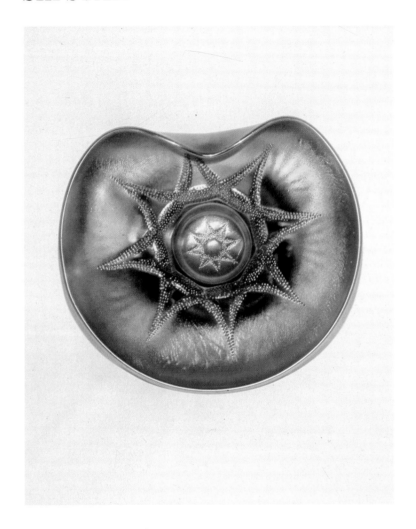

While Ski Star is found occasionally on small bowls in purple, blue and green, it is on the larger dome-footed bowls in peach opalescent where the pattern has its "day in the sun". These are found in many variations, some crimpled with one side turned down, others with both sides pulled up to resemble a banana bowl.

The exterior usually carries the Compass pattern, an interesting geometric design, or is plain.

STORK AND RUSHES

Stork and Rushes is another pattern whose shards were found in the Dugan diggings and since it has features that are typical of Northwood, I'm afraid it's difficult to state whether Dugan or Northwood made this pattern.

At any rate, it is available in berry sets, punch sets, water sets, hats and mugs.

I've seen only marigold, purple and blue with purple probably the hardest color to find.

SUPERB DRAPE

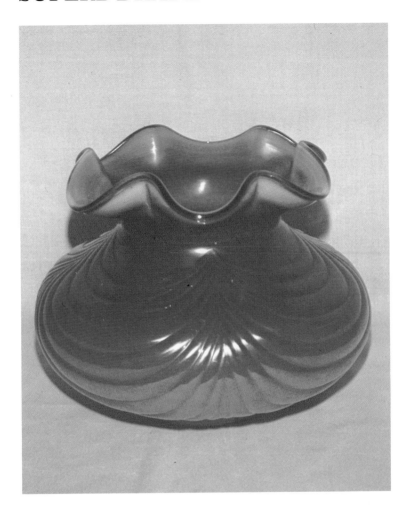

The title of this beautiful piece of glass is certainly appropriate -it is superb!

About 6½'' tall and 7'' in diameter, this very rare vase is a true aqua with a rich even butterscotch iridization. The gently rolling top shows a mellow opalescence as does the base.

All in all, a rare beauty that would grace any collection superbly!

SWAN, PASTEL

Of all the shards of patterns I catalogued from the Dugan dump site, I'm sure this pattern surprised me more than any other.

For years I considered these small novelties either Fenton or Westmoreland products with my vote leaning toward the latter. However, we now can say with some positiveness they are either Dugan or Northwood.

Found in pink, ice blue, ice green, marigold, peach and purple, the darker colors and peach are the scarcest and demand greater prices.

THREE ROW VASE*

   I was very impressed when I saw this beautiful rarity. The color was truly fabulous and the iridesence fine enough to rivel the Farmyard bowl.
   I have heard of only this one piece in beautiful purple, but others may exist. It is 8'' tall and 4½'' wide and the mold work is quite deep and sharp.
   There is also a varient called *Two Row* vase which is quite similar.

*Now known to be an Imperial pattern

VICTORIAN

Let me say in the beginning I think this is one of the most under-rated patterns in the entire field of carnival glass.

In size it is generous and commanding being some 11'' in diameter.

Also, the glass is heavy, the color is deep and rich while the iridescence often rivals that of the Farmyard bowl.

Indeed, I can not understand why it doesn't bring raves since it is relatively scarce and always adds a great deal of class to any collection.

Purple is the only color I've ever seen.

VINEYARD

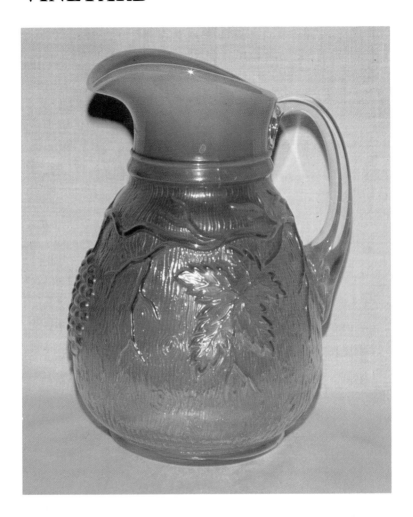

Here is another pattern whose shards I catalogued from the Dugan diggings, but actually it didn't come as too much of a surprise. The same design was made in 1905 in crystal, opaque glass and opalescent wear under the name, Grape and Leaf. (See Heacock-Book II, pp 26).

Known in iridescent glass, in a water set only, the colors are marigold, purple and rarely peach opalescent. Often the tumblers are poorly formed and the glass tends toward being bubbled.

WINDFLOWER

Not one but two shards of this pattern were excavated at the Dugan site, including a marigold bit and a sizeable chunk of an ice blue nappy with a portion of the handle attached. To the best of my knowledge, this pattern has not been reported previously in pastels.

Windflower is an uncomplicated, well balanced design with the background stippled and a geometric bordering device. The exterior is plain.

Windflower is found on bowls, plates and handled nappies. The colors are marigold, cobalt and ice blue.

WOODPECKER VASE

I certainly wouldn't have considered this pattern as a possible Northwood product if I hadn't catalogued a rather sizeable hunk from the Dugan diggings.

The Woodpecker vase is 8 1/4'' long and measures 1 5/8'' across the top. The only color I've run into is marigold, usually of good color.

Perhaps this is strictly a Dugan pattern, and if so, it would explain the lack of other colors or shapes.

These vases were usually hung in doorways or used as auto vases and were quite popular in their day.

WREATHED CHERRY

For many years, collectors have been puzzled by certain pieces of this pattern turning up with the Diamond Glass Company trademark, notably the covered butter.

Now, since the Dugan shards have been catalogued, it becomes apparent this was a Dugan pattern.

Known in berry sets, consisting of oval bowls, table sets, water sets and a scarce toothpick holder, the colors are marigold, fiery amethyst, purple and white (often with gilt).

The toothpick has been widely reproduced in cobalt, white and marigold, so beware! The only color in the old ones is amethyst.

WREATH OF ROSES ROSEBOWL

I've never understood why this little rosebowl has been grouped with the Fenton Wreath of Roses as *one and the same pattern* when it is obviously so different.

So when a large hunk of Wreath of Roses Rosebowl was found among the Dugan shards, the explanation became obvious. They simply are not the same pattern!

Found in marigold and amethyst, the Wreath of Roses Rosebowl has very superior mold work and adequate finish.

ZIPPERED HEART*

Here is another heavy, well-done geometric so often found in the glass field.

Zippered Heart is available on berry sets (usually with plain interiors), water sets and a large vase shape known as a Queen's Vase.

The colors are marigold, green and a very rich amethyst.

*Now known to be an Imperial pattern.

PRICE INDEX

Again we arrive at that necessary evil, the price guide.

I'm sure you will find it pretty much self-explanatory. All prices are for *mint* items and damaged glass or poor iridescence decreases the value.

The opalescent column includes both Peach and Aqua (two colors very high on the popularity list of collectors).

Finally, let me say that carnival glass has "weathered the storm" and has proven itself to be an excellent investment. The average pattern increases in value at a moderate but constant rate while the rarities climb in great strides. Anyone who attended the Wishard auction in 1977 is aware of this, for not only were record prices recorded on rarities, but standard patterns often went for premium amounts.

I'm sure this price guide won't please everyone; none ever could. But please remember it isn't the last word but only a *guide*. The real price guide is still supply and demand.

COLOR CODE:

A	-	Amethyst
B	-	Blue
G	-	Green
P	-	Purple
M	-	Marigold
PO	-	Peach Opalescent
AO	-	Aqua Opalescent
IG	-	Ice Green
IB	-	Ice Blue
W	-	White
EB	-	Electric Blue
C	-	Clear Carnival

PRICE INDEX

	Mar.	Dark	Aqua Peach Opal	Pastels
ACORN BURRS				
10" Bowl	75.	125.		225.
5" Bowl	20.	28.		40.
Punch Bowl and Base	275.	475.		2200.IB
Punch Cups	18.	27.		40.
Covered Butter	90.	180.		220.
Covered Sugar	75.	90.		125.
Creamer or Spooner	65.	80.		100.
Pitcher, Water	185.	400.		
Tumbler	40.	50.		
ADVERTISING ITEMS				
Various Shapes and Prices				
Too Numerous to List				
AMARYLLIS				
Compote	75.			
APPLE BLOSSOMS				
Bowl 7" - 9½"	22.	38.	50.PO	50.
Plate 7½" - 9"	75.	90.		100.
APPLE BLOSSOM TWIGS				
Bowl 7" - 9½"	40.	50.	45.PO	60.
Plate 8" - 9"	60.	98.	85.PO	110.
BASKET				
One shape	50.	70.	325.AO	160.W
BASKETWEAVE				
Compote		48.		
BEADED CABLE				
Rosebowl FTD	50.	75.	290.AO	95.
Candy Dish FTD	40.	65.	285.AO	75.
BEADS				
Bowl 8" - 9"	35.	55.		
BEADED SHELL				
Berry - Lg. Bowl FTD	60.	135.		
Small Bowl FTD	28.	40.		
Mug	50.	75.P		
FTD Covered Butter	110.	160.		
FTD Covered Sugar	75.	90.		
FTD Creamer or Spooner	60.	80.		
Water Pitcher	350.	450.		
Tumbler	70.	90.		
BEAUTY BUD VASE				
5" - 9" tall	25.	38.		50.
Twig size - Rare		175.		
BIG BASKETWEAVE				
Vase 6" - 12"	18.	28.	35.PO	80.W
Basket - Small	25.			

PRICE INDEX

	Mar.	Dark	Aqua Peach Opal	Pastels
BLACKBERRY				
FTD Compote (Lg.)	35.	50.		90.
Small Stemmed Compote	32.	45.		
BLOSSOMTIME				
Compote	50.	90.		75.
BULL'S EYE AND BEADS				
Vase	25.	50.		
BULL'S EYE AND LEAVES				
Bowl 8'' - 9½''	28.	50.		
BUTTERFLY				
Bon Bon	38.	60.		135.IB
BUTTERFLY AND TULIP				
Large FTD Bowl - Scarce	275.	1075.		
CHERRY				
Bowls 7½'' - 9'' FTD	28.	40.	48.PO	
Bowls Flat - 6''	18.	26.		
Bowls Flat - 9''	28.	58.		
CHERRY AND CABLE (Thumbprint)				
Berry Bowl 9''	65.			
Small Bowl 5''	30.			
Covered Butter	200.			
Covered Sugar	110.			
Creamer or Spooner	80.			
Tumbler	190.			
Pitcher	750.			
COIN SPOT				
Compote	22.	35.	170.AO	50.
CONSTELLATION				
Compote	22.	35.	50.PO	45.
CORINTH				
Bowl 8'' - 9''			65.	
Banana Plate	30.	45.	150.PO	
Vase 6½'' - 10''	18.	27.	90.PO	40.
CORN VASE				
Regular	300.	275.		190.IG
Pulled Husk - Rare		700.		
DAHLIA				
Berry Bowl Lg. FTD	90.	130.		250.W
Bowl Small	20.	38.		90.W
Covered Butter	90.	150.		300.W
Covered Sugar	60.	90.		250.W
Creamer - Spooner	50.	80.		220.W
Water Pitcher	460.	650.		900.W
Tumbler	65.	80.		350.W

PRICE INDEX

	Mar.	Dark	Aqua Peach Opal	Pastels
DAISY AND DRAPE				
Vase	95.	150.	300.AO	110.W
DAISY AND PLUME				
Compote				
Candy Dish	20.	30.		55.
Rose Bowl	28.	45.		60.
DANDELION				
Mug	300.	300.	500.AO	350.
Tankard Pitcher	385.	575.		1000.
Tumbler	40.	70.		160.
DIAMOND POINT				
Vase	18.	28.	30.PO	40.
DOGWOOD SPRAYS				
Compote	35.		50.PO	
Bowl - Dome FTD 8" - 9½"		55.	65.PO	
DRAPERY				
Rose Bowl	50.	70.		85.
Candy Dish		70.		60.
Vase	22.	38.	40.PO	40.
EMBROIDERED MUMS				
Bon-Bon				87.
Bowl 8½" - 9½"	38.	55.		75.
FAN				
Sauce	20.	35.		
Occasional Piece	38.	85.	75.PO	85.C
FANCIFUL				
Bowls 8" - 9½"	28.	48.	55.PO	65.
Plate - Rare	85.	130.		
FANCY				
Interior Pattern		2300.P		
FARMYARD				
Bowl - Rare		6000. Green	10,000PO	
FEATHERS				
Vase	16.	28.		35.
FERN				
Compote	28.	45.		60.
Bowl - 7" - 8½"	26.	40.		
Hat Shape	48.	70.		80.
FINE CUT AND ROSES				
Rose Bowl FTD	38.	68.	300.AO	75.
Candy Dish FTD	32.	45.		55.

PRICE INDEX

	Mar.	Dark	Aqua Peach Opal	Pastels
FINE RIB				
Vase	18.	30.	32.PO	37.
Bowl 9'' - 10½''		55.		
Bowl 5''		26.		
Plate 8'' - 9''	60.	85.	90.PO	110.
FIVE HEARTS				
Bowl - Dome FTD		48.	55.PO	
FLUTE				
Covered Butter	65.	85.		
Open Sugar	40.	60.		
Creamer-Spooner	38.	55.		
Compote		40.		
Pitcher	300.	480.		
Tumbler	35.	45.		
FRUITS AND FLOWERS				
Bon Bon - Stemmed	28.	45.	195.AO	60.
Bowl 9'' - 10''	38.	55.		75.
Bowl - 5''	22.	35.		45.
Plate 7'' - 9½''	45.	85.		110.
GARDEN PATH & VT.				
Bowl 8'' - 9½''	32.	55.	90.PO	60.
Compote - Rare	185.	245.		390.
Fruit Bowl - 10'' - 11''		110.	140.PO	110.
Plate 7''	210.	285.	300.PO	
Plate 10'' - 11'' - Rare		1800.	1500.	
GOOD LUCK				
Bowl 8½'' - 9½''	65.	95.		135.
Plate 9''	125.	185.		250.
GRACEFUL				
Vase Only	35.	65.		70.
GRAPE (and Cable)				
Berry Bowl 9'' - 10'' Thumbprints	65.	85.		120
Small Bowl 5½'' Thumprints	20.	32.		48.
Scalloped Bowls 5'' - 11½''	40.	70.		85.
Bon Bon	32.	55.		80.
Banana Boat FTD	200.	185.		300.
Bowl Flt. 7'' - 9''	35.	45.		
Ice Cream Bowl 11''	95.	185.		240.
Orange Bowl FTD	125.	175.	2600.AO	1300.IG
Breakfast Set - Two pieces	110.	160.		
Candlesticks - Pair	170.	260.		400.
Compote Lg. Covered	2000.	500.		
Compote Lg. Open	450.	350.		600.
Sweetmeat - Covered	425.	250.		
Cookie Jar - Covered	350.	375.	900.AO	400.
FTD Centerpiece Bowl	285.	380.		500.
Cup and Saucer Set - Rare		310.		
Cologne w/stopper	125.	110.		300.

PRICE INDEX

	Mar.	Dark	Aqua Peach Opal	Pastels
Perfume w/stopper	400.	450.		
Dresser Tray	140.	185.		280.
Pin Tray	110.	155.		230.
Hatpin Holder	230.	210.	2000.AO	300.
Powder Jar w/Lid	55.	70.	300.AO	
Nappy	70.	85.		120.
Fernery - FTD - Rare	1350.	750.		2500.IB
Hat	35.	58.		110.
Ice Cream Sherbet	35.	48.		90.
Plate 6'' - 9½'' Flat	65.	85.		105.
Plate Handgrip	58.	75.		90.
Plate FTD	78.	90.		120.
Plate Two Sides Up	50.	68.		
Shade for Lamp	185.	160.		
Punch Bowl and Base - Banquet	1500.	2100.P	7500.AO	3700.
Punch Bowl and Base - Standard Rare	500.	800.		950.
Punch Bowl and Base - Small	300.	400.		525.
Cup, Punch	28.	35.	185.AO	42.
Covered Butter	165.	235.		475.
Covered Sugar	78.	165.		240.
Creamer-Spooner	65.	145.		190.
Tobacco Jar w/Lid	385.	400.		
Pitcher - Water	285.	375.		390.
Pitcher - Tankard	875.	800.		
Tumbler - Jumbo	48.	72.		95.
Tumbler - Regular	35.	58.		70.
Whiskey Decanter	850.	975.		
Shot Glass	155.	185.		
Spittoon - Rare	4800.	7000.P		
Orange Bowl Basket - Very Rare		2750.		

GRAPE AND GOTHIC ARCHES

	Mar.	Dark	Aqua Peach Opal	Pastels
Berry Bowl, Lg.	38.	55.		
Bowl 5''	22.	38.		
Covered Butter	75.	95.		
Covered Sugar	50.	65.		
Creamer - Spooner	40.	55.		
Water Pitcher	195.	295.		
Tumbler	26.	38.		

GRAPE ARBOR

	Mar.	Dark	Aqua Peach Opal	Pastels
Bowl FTD - 9½'' - 11''	135.	195.		220.
Hat Shape - Scarce	45.	85.B		75.
Tankard Pitcher	195.	500.		2500.IG
Tumbler	35.	60.		125.IG

GRAPE DELIGHT

	Mar.	Dark	Aqua Peach Opal	Pastels
Rose Bowl	45.	55.		65.W
Nut Bowl - Rare		65.P		

GRAPE LEAVES

	Mar.	Dark	Aqua Peach Opal	Pastels
Bowl 7½'' - 9½''	45.	65.		125.IB

PRICE INDEX

	Mar.	Dark	Aqua Peach Opal	Pastels
GRAPEVINE LATTICE				
Plate 7" - 8"	40.	58.		65.W
Bowl 7" - 8"	23.	38.		50.W
Tankard Pitcher	185.	400.		650.W
Tumbler	35.	55.		50.W
GREEK KEY & VT				
Bowl FTD or Flat	75.	95.		
Plate	185.	250.		
Pitcher Rare	700.	950.		1000.
Tumbler Rare	65.	95.		115.
HEARTS AND FLOWERS				
Bowl 8" - 9½"	40.	65.	250.AO	80.
Compote	45.	75.	275.AO	90.
Plate - 9" - 10" -Rare	125.	250.		285.
HEAVY IRIS				
Pitcher	450.	1100.		1200.W
Tumbler	90.	130.		150.W
HEAVY WEB				
Bowls 9" - 11"			125.PO	
HOBSTAR FLOWER				
Compote - Rare	60.	75.		
HOLIDAY				
Tray - 11" - Rare	185.			
HOLLY AND BERRY				
Handled Nappy	45.	65.	85.PO	
Bowl	35.	50.	65.PO	
HOLLY, PANELLED				
Bowl		50.		
Bon Bon FTD	38.	48.		
Water Pitcher - Very Rare		9000.A		
IDYLL				
Vase - Rare		285.		
INTERIOR POINSETTIA				
Tumbler - Rare	450.			
JEWELLED HEART				
Berry Bowl 9" - 10½"		90.	85.PO	
Berry Bowl 5"		42.	32.PO	
Pitcher Rare	625.			
Tumbler Rare	85.			500.W
JOCKEY CLUB				
Plate		125.		
KNIGHT'S TEMPLER MUG - Rare				
(Dandelion) Advertising	420.			500.

PRICE INDEX

	Mar.	Dark	Aqua Peach Opal	Pastels
LEAF AND BEADS				
Rose Bowl - FTD	45.	65.	210.AO	100.
Candy Bowl - FTD	38.	54.	185.AO	100.
LEAF COLUMN				
Vase	28.	35.	55.PO	44.
Shade				95.
LOVELY				
Bowl	110.	185.P		
LUSTRE FLUTE				
Bowl 7½" - 8½"	18.	25.		
Bon-Bon		32.		
Compote		28.		
Creamer-Sugar	34.	39.		
Hat	18.	30.		
Nappy	20.	28.		
Punch Bowl and Base		165.		
Cup	12.	16.		
Sherbet	18.	27.		
MANY FRUITS				
Punch Bowl and Base	165.	250.		750.W
Cups	18.	26.		35.W
MAPLE LEAF				
Lg. Ice Cream Bowl - Stemmed	55.	110.		
Small Ice Cream Bowl - Stemmed	15.	28.		
Covered Butter	85.	110.		
Covered Sugar	50.	65.		
Creamer-Spooner - Each	38.	50.		
Pitcher	135.	285.		
Tumbler	25.	38.		
MEMPHIS				
Lg. Berry Bowl	60.	90.		
Sm. Berry Bowl	20.	40.		
Compote		110.		
Fruit Bowl and Base	110.	160.		500.IB
Punch Bowl and Base	160.	240.		580.IB
Cup	22.	32.		40.IB
NAUTILIS				
Compote - Rare		185.	220.PO	
Giant Compote - Very Rare	1000.			
NEAR-CUT				
Compote		90.P		
Goblet	80.	110.P		
Pitcher - Very Rare	1400.			
NIPPON				
Bowl 8½" - 9½"	40.	58.		100.

PRICE INDEX

	Mar.	Dark	Aqua Peach Opal	Pastels
OCTET				
FTD Bowl - 8½" - 9½"	38.	55.		65.
ORIENTAL POPPY				
Tankard Pitcher	400.	650.		1000.
Tumbler	30.	40.		150.IB
PEACH				
Berry Bowl 9" - 10"				195.W
Berry Bowl 5½"				45.W
Covered Butter				200.W
Covered Sugar				95.W
Creamer or Spooner		65.		65.W
Pitcher		525.B		600.W
Tumbler		75.B		85.W
PEACOCKS				
Bowl 8" - 9½"	70.	90.	400.AO	185.
Plate 9"	100.	135.	485.AO	210.
PETAL AND FAN				
Bowls	42.	95.	57.PO	65.
PEACOCK AND URN				
Bowl 9"	55.	85.	310.AO	90.
Bowl 11" Ice Cream	145.	210.	675.AO	460.
Bowl 5"	30.	45.		55.
Plate 9"	275.	600.		750.
Plate 11½"		850.		
PEACOCK AT FOUNTAIN				
Berry Bowl - Lg.	58.	90.		165.
Berry Bowl - Small	22.	30.		55.
Orange Bowl - FTD...............	120.	175.	3000.AO	285.
Shade - Rare				140.
Punch Bowl and Base	150.	310.	3500.AO	395.
Cup..........................	18.	26.	150.AO	36.
Covered Butter	95.	145.		195.
Covered Sugar	60.	85.		110.
Creamer or Spooner	50.	70.		95.
Compote.......................	135.	235.	285.AO	250.
Pitcher	235.	385.P		550.
Tumbler	26.	52.P		65.
POINSETTIA				
Bowl - Flat or Footed	85.	135.		175.W
POPPY				
Bowl 7" - 8½"	45.	55.	85.PO	
Oval Pickle Tray	48.	60.		75.
Dresser Tray-Flat - Rare		200.EB		225.
PRISMS				
Compote.......................	55.	75.		100.-Aqua

PRICE INDEX

	Mar.	Dark	Aqua Peach Opal	Pastels
PUMP, TOWN				
Occasional Piece	675.	700.G 550.A		
QUESTION MARKS				
Bon Bon	22.	32.	32.PO	40.
Compote-Scarce	25.	40.	45.PO	55.
QUILL				
Pitcher - Rare...................	1500.	3000.P		
Tumbler - Rare	250.	450.P		
RAINDROPS				
Bowl Dome FTD		95.P	58.PO	
RAMBLER ROSE				
Pitcher	145.	190.		
Tumbler	25.	37.		
RASPBERRY				
Berry Bowl 9"	38.	57.		
Berry Bowl 5½"	22.	28.		
Milk Pitcher....................	110.	135.		1500.IB
Occasional Piece, FTD	68.	85.		
Pitcher	125.	185.		1900.IB
Tumbler	25.	38.		150.IB
ROSE SHOW & VT				
Bowl 8½" - 9½"	125.	175.	395.	225.
Plate 8½" - 9¾"	165.	275.	550.AO	285.
ROSETTE				
Bowl	40.	75.		
ROUND-UP				
Bowl - 9"	48.	70.	55.PO	85.
Plate - 9¼" FTD or Ruffled	110.	145.	135.PO	160.
S-REPEAT				
Creamer - Rare		85.		
Punch Bowl and Base - Rare		1200.		
Punch Cup		35.		
Toothpick Holder-Rare		210.	Purple Only	
Tumbler-Age questionable..........	125.			
SCALES				
Bowl 8" - 9½"	18.	37.	270.AO	40.
Plate 6" - 9"	32.	55.	40.PO	58.
SINGING BIRDS				
Berry Bowl 10"	45.	55.		
Berry Bowl 5"	28.	20.		
Mug...........................	125.	75.P		900.IB
Covered Butter	185.	185.		
Covered Sugar	50.	50.		

	Mar.	Dark	Aqua Peach Opal	Pastels
Spooner - Creamer, Each	50.	50.		
Pitcher	170.	185.		
Tumbler	30.	35.		
SIX PETALS				
Plate 7" - 9" - Rare			58.PO	150.
Bowl 8" - 9½"	18.	28.	175.PO	40.
SKI-STAR				
Berry Bowl 9" - 11"	42.	75.	55.PO	
Berry Bowl - 5½"	20.	35.	27.PO	
Banana Bowl Dome FTD		95.	175.PO	
SPRINGTIME				
Berry Bowl 9"		85.		
Berry Bowl 5"		35.		
Covered Butter	125.	185.		
Covered Sugar	80.	110.		
Spooner, Creamer	80.	110.		
Water Pitcher - Rare	400.	900.		975.
Tumbler - Rare	55.	75.		95.
STAR OF DAVID AND BOWS				
Bowl FTD 8½" - 9½"	38.	50.		68.
STIPPLED RAYS & VTS				
Bowl	38.	55.		
Bon-Bon	24.	35.		
STORK AND RUSHES				
Berry Bowl 10"	37.	52.		
Berry Bowl 5"	16.	24.		
Mug	26.	90.		
Punch Bowl and Base	130.	175.		
Punch Cup	12.	25.		
Hat	16.	28.		
Pitcher	190.	285.		
Tumbler	18.	28.		
STRAWBERRY				
Bowl 9½"	37.	45.		150.W
Bowl 5½"	16.	18.		
Plate 9"	70.	85.		
Hand Grip Plate 8"	60.	75.		
STRAWBERRY INTAGLIO				
Bowls - 10"	28.			
Bowls - 5"	12.			
SUNFLOWER				
Bowl 8½" - 9½"	28.	47.		65.
Plate	140.	285.		
SUPERB DRAPE				
Rose Bowl			500.AO	

PRICE INDEX

	Mar.	Dark	Aqua Peach Opal	Pastels
SWAN, PASTEL				
One Shape	45.	75.P	65.PO	28.
SWIRL				
Pitcher	125.			
Tumbler	35.	45.		
Mug - Rare	50.			
THREE FRUITS				
Bowl 9½"	28.	48.		
Bowl 5½"	16.	24.		
Bon-Bon - Stemmed	32.	48.		60.
Plate 9"	72.	90.	350.AO	
THREE ROW VASES				
Rare		350.P		
TORNADO				
Vase - Smooth or Ribbed	125.	105.		200.IB
TREE TRUNK				
Vase 7" - 22"	22.	38.UP		45.UP
Jardeniere - Whimsey - Rare		250.		
TWO FRUITS				
Spooner - Very Rare		400.B		
Sugar - Very Rare		400.B		
VICTORIAN				
Bowl 10" - 12"		175.P		
VINEYARD				
Pitcher	65.	185.	450.PO	
Tumbler	12.	30.		145.W
WATERLILY AND CATTAILS				
Bowl 9½"	45.	65.		
Bowl 5½"	25.	38.		
Covered Butter	125.			
Sugar	80.			
Creamer, Spooner-Each	80.			
Pitcher	585.			
Tumbler	85.			
WHEAT				
Bowl - Very Rare		2500.		
Sweetmeat w/lid - Very Rare		2500.		
WILD ROSE				
Bowl - Reg. edge	18.	30.		350.IB
Bowl - Open edge	24.	40.G		
WILD STRAWBERRY				
Bowl - 8" - 10½"		110.		200.W
Plate 7" - 9"		200.		

PRICE INDEX

	Mar.	Dark	Aqua Peach Opal	Pastels
WINDFLOWER				
Bowl 8½'' - 9½''	22.	37.		
Plate 9''	65.	110.		
Nappy-Handled..................	26.			55.IB
WISHBONE				
Bowl 8½'' - 9½'' Flat or Footed	40.	65.		85.
Epergne - One Lily		175.		225.IB
Plate - 9'' Footed.................		300.		
Plate - 10'' Flat		400.		
Pitcher - Rare....................	800.	1900.		
Tumbler	60.	85.		
WISTERIA				
Pitcher - Rare....................				3800.
Tumbler - Rare				600.
WOODPECKER				
Vase	28.			
WREATH OF ROSES				
Rose Bowl	35.	50.		
WREATHED CHERRY				
Oval Berry Bowl - Large...........	65.	85.		250.W
Oval Berry Bowl - Small...........	18.	27.		85.W
Covered Butter	85.	140.		175.W
Creamer, Sugar, Spooner, Each	60.	100.		120.W
Toothpick *Old Only*		150.		
Pitcher	145.	485.		810.W
Tumbler	30.	45.		60.W
ZIPPERED HEART				
Berry Bowl 9½''	50.	85.		
Berry Bowl 5½''	20.	30.		
Pitcher - Very Rare	350.	900.		
Tumbler - Very Rare	45.	95.		
Queen's Vase - Rare		650.		

2812-7
5-34
C